Iron to Irony

The Show

Written and Performed

by JANUL

Copyright © 2021, Jan Knox (JANUL), Janul Publications
ISBN: 978-1-906921-02-6

JANUL

07850 846495 **jan@janul.com** **www.janul.com**

NOTE:- Videos are used for promotion of the show but none are used in live performances

IRON to IRONY is a lively, solo musical show, written and performed by JANUL.

Experience the "observations" of BCN108 (Joe) from the time of her launch to the present day, but also witness the development of modern boating, with its cruisers, widebeams and indeed, the canal itself.

Consisting of original songs and stories from over 40 years of boat antics, JANUL has an enthusistic dialogue, with more than a hint of tonque in cheek humour.

You will be carried along on a journey which declares both passion and emotion for the people and boats that JANUL has met through her own life, work and travels.

The performance is loosely scripted and open to audience participation, which helps to make every performance unique.

The show is flexible towards large or small venues, indoor or outside performances (weather permitting) and uses PA where appropriate.

The full show including interval is 2 hours but timing can be flexible.

It is suitable for all ages, although some funny songs about boat toilets are carefully administered with gentleness to the unitiated or fragile.

Some performances are ticketed, but JANUL is happy to work for "pass the hat" donations, so that everyone can afford to be included.

Kindness and inclusion bring the greatest rewards of the heart.

I am very much looking forward to meeting you.

JANUL

BCN108 (Joe), was launched in 1883, with a fairly short life expectency.
She began her life as a horseboat on the Birmingham canals

Perhaps it is ironic that this iron "Joey" boat has outlived many of her steerers.
She will live on into the future, leaving her current custodian long behind.

Share Joe's story and her tales of the modern canal, and see a very different outcome.

Sing along with the songs depicting her life and the lives of other boats,
as the show travels through time and into another millenium.

Joey Reprise - Part One

Far in the past
Your existence was born
Oh, how you toiled
You became weatherworn
Life it was hard
As you weathered the storm
Some days be merry
But some were forlorn

Still carrying cargo
Along waterway
More than one King or Queen
Passed in your day
1914
Sent the Great War your way
Then came the Depression
A time long and grey

Seems like we hadn't seen
War to end wars
On came the next one
With barely a pause
Women stepped into jobs
Little applause
Men off to fight again
All for the cause

Iron to Irony

I am Iron
I am warm and living
And I am from another time

Steel or wood, Fibreglass, Even concrete
These are my Sisters
Who float beside me
And I am amongst the oldest
Of them all

For I am Iron
I am warm and living
And I am from another time

Keep The Joeys Moving

Old Ned, his head it nodded; Down the BCN we plodded
We worked the boats from morn until the night
The Gaffer kept us working, no room round here for shirking
He'd sack us if we didn't get things right
You had to be quite humble and if you start to grumble
Your mate would tell you straight to keep it shut
And gently intertwined, several boats were towed behind
As we kept the Joeys moving down the cut

Well, engines came along and we had to change the song
We missed old Ned but change it had to come
The Gaffer, Lord and Master, said get the work done faster
The engine was the way to get things done
We had to get her going as the swear words started flowing
I admit the Vicar often had to tut
At least it kept us jolly, working with the Bolly
As we kept the joeys moving down the cut

The Company was rough, work was dangerous and tough
And we nearly met the angels up above
But as long as we was able to put bread on the table
We had a life that earned respect and love
The weather came and went with no need for our consent
In the sweet Black Country air of soot and smut
And as the years went by, made us laugh and made us cry
As we kept the joeys moving down the cut

CHORUS
Keep the joeys moving, keep the joeys moving
Keep the joeys moving down the cut
Keep the joeys moving, keep the joeys moving
Keep the joeys moving down the cut

The Coalboats Are Coming

It's dark and it's cold, winter is old
Gas and the coal running low
Keep a look out, for there's little doubt
That they'll get here through ice and through snow
What's that I hear? There's no need to fear
As they battle the bridge to get through
Don't argue for space, if there is a race
Well you know they'll be winning that too

The boats have arrived and all have survived
The dangers they met on the way
But don't fall in the water
'cos if that boat caught yer
You'd likely not see the next day
In time honoured ways
They are spending their days
Tradition so unchanged by men
The coalboats are here
So give them good cheer
Or they might not come back here again

Chorus

The Coalboats are coming
The Coalboats are coming
There's nothing to stand in their way
The Coalboats are coming
The Coalboats are coming
They're gonna be through here today

A different breed of working boat covered long routes and families lived aboard in tiny cabins.

Some of these boats are still working today

CREDIT: Photo: British Waterways

During world war 2, ladies took over the roles of our boatmen as part of the war effort, the "landgirls of the water".

They wore a badge with the initials "IW", standing for "Inland Waterways" and were often, (by some), known as the "Idle Women".

Of course, they were anything but idle and eventually, after much hard work and perseverance, they became an integral part of the working boat community.

When the war ended, the boatmen returned and women went back to their normal lives and their own families, often with wistful longing for the life which they no longer needed to endure.

"Idle" Women

CHORUS
Idle Women, Inland Waterways was the badge they wore
Idle Women, living the life they'd never known before
Idle Women, working in weather that chilled them to the core
Days were good and days were bad, some were happy and some were sad, living the life the boatmen had
As England went to war

Well, it was very hard at first, the boatmen thought it wrong
That ladies coming from the bank could feel that they belong
But trust it grew and friendships new grew bonds which were so strong
Company in times forlorn, teaching kids from pages torn
Helping hands when babes were born as England went to war

Now, people didn't understand when women ventured home
Why comradeship and hardship meant you'd never be alone
Why backbreaking war effort didn't seem a cause to moan
Dirty filthy can't complain, table manners down the drain
Couldn't wait to get back again when England went to war

So VE day it came and went and sadness came around
No more camaraderie or engines constant pound
Memories were all they had and to their hearts were bound
Loved the life for all its sins, money kept in treacle tins
Engines fixed with safety pins as England went to war

Joey Reprise - Part Two

Trains came along and left little to see
Canals that aren't used they decline easily
Purpose was gone as the cargo did flee
No choice but to set all the working boats free

Spent many years in enforced solitude
Full of the rubbish which kept you subdued
With Volunteer labour your life was renewed
Restoring canal owes them much gratitude

Narrowboats, cruisers for holiday trade
Workboats still seen with their cargoes displayed
Leisurely waterway, memories made
Always kept moving on, never afraid

Don't Mess Me Around

Well, my name is Ernie Fiddler and I'm only 16 feet
I get some strange reactions from the people that I meet
They like to prod and poke my sides as if I am not real
"Hey Geezer, get your hands off, I'm not there for you to feel"

Chorus
So, don't mess me around, or I'll have you in the lock
'specially if you're plastic, just like a little yoghurt pot
Don't mess me around, 'cos I really am quite real
I am a proper leisure boat made out of proper steel

I can match your attitude, my steel is just as thick
Just because you're longer, don't try and take the Mick
Don't push past me for the lock, prepare to do your worst
Just get behind me, take your turn, 'cos I was in here first

My engine is respectable, a Petter with one pot
It's obvious when you look at me the breeding that I've got
I wear the family livery, so don't you get me wrong
Or I'll let you meet my sister Mo – she's 70 foot long

Some things never change as the locks go ever on and on

The locks go ever, ever on	The locks go ever, ever on	The locks go ever, ever on
Over hills	Beneath the cloud	As lifted on
Far as you see	& twinkling star	Our narrow way
Through gates where	& those who up	When summit reached
Many more have gone	The hill have gone	& junctions meet
The way ahead	Find what looks near	Decide -
So wild & free	Can be so far	Where shall we go today?
Winter passes	Through view that flyboat	So let our journey
Breeze hath blown	Once had seen	New begin
More people here	We feel the strain	For troubles deep
In heat of June	Of flesh & bone	From which we ran
& many worry	As looking up	Are far behind
Many moan	With envy green	And sun has shone
That flight-end	Boat getting to	Into this life
Isn't coming soon	The top is shown	Since we began
The locks go ever on and on	The locks go ever on and on	The locks go ever on and on
The locks go ever on and on	The locks go ever on and on	The locks go ever on and on

Like A Storm

Chorus
Like A Storm, you came into my life
Like I'd never been born, like I'd never lived before
Like a Storm, you expanded the scene, places I'd never been
And you made me what I am, 'cos I can - Like a Storm

I asked for a wish and you placed the whole world in my hand
You never deceived me, your promises fluid as sand
You promised me dreams that were deep in my mind
Never explaining just what I would find
I wish that you'd said life was sometimes unkind

It wasn't as easy as I led the story to be
Pure desolation, the loneliest places I'd see
Look up at the heavens, this doesn't seem right
Hang on, keep climing, the end is in sight
Nearing the top now and seeing the light

Every "Joey" appreciates her Tug and
Joe and Storm are a great partnership.

Photograph by Mark Rogers

Hello there, I'm a widebeam, I'd like to come & play
& though I know I'm very young I'll not get in the way
I know I don't have heritage or long slim form like you
But I'm really very keen to learn the things that you can do

I'm very new & shiny so spare a second glance
I'm also big and very square but give me half a chance
I'm very much a travelling girl and it can't be so wrong
To want to meet the other boats and feel that I belong

You tease my need to "bow thrust" to try & keep me straight
But thrusters stop me hitting things & I think that's just great
'cos steering me needs different skills, I'm hoping you can see
My owner's trying hard to steer this great big thing called "Me"

So if you see me on the cut a smile upon my face
Just say hello and let me moor there with you – (if there's space)
And please be patient with me, I wear my width with pride
I try so hard at fitting in but sometimes I'm too wide

Widebeam

CHORUS
Yes, I'm wide
I'm not so long & thin
I'm just a very young widebeam
Trying my hardest to fit in

Look For The Coalboats

They loaded tons of unbagged coal, it nearly broke your back
They used to use a shovel as they stuffed it in a sack
But now it comes in plastic in the ultra-modern way
Pity it's as heavy as in Uncle Archies day

They're climbing on the coalbags as they throw them up to you
& sharing out the coaldust so that you'll be filthy too
& if you want some diesel, well, they'll get some from their stash
Gas bottles and some kindling wood are there if you've got cash

'twas on a fine May morning the coalman did appear
Came cruising through the morning mist, a fag behind his ear
He said, "you got the kettle on?" I said "do it yourself"
He said, "when you've moved 40 bags your gas is on the shelf"

Their services are many, there is nothing they won't do
And if you've got a porta-pot, they'll tip it out for you
But if you have a holding tank it's contents they will lift
They'll stick the little pipe in and your ballast they will shift

**Chorus
Look for the coalboats
A memory of the past
& if you see a working boat
It might be your last
So get your muscles ready
As you help the coal ashore
The coalman & his coalboat
Will deliver to your door**

The stories of the boats are intertwined with the people who love them

If you fall in love with the lifestyle it will never let you go

How Can I Ever Repay

You've been here for such a long time
But how could I know
When I didn't know who you were
How could I let it show
That one day I'd need you to pick up
The shattered pieces of my life
Never knowing how well
You'd free me from trouble and strife

And what of tomorrow?
Who will we be?
Will you be who you are now?
Will I be me?
Will we be together?
Who could possibly say?
All I know is that I'm thankful to you
& I'd like to be with you today

So how can I ever repay you
For spreading light upon my way
For showing me the truth read so clearly from my eyes
Lifting the shadows, allowing the sun to rise again in my life

Let's Have another Drink

This boating life is full of fun, especially when it's in the sun
But life's not always full of cheer, 'specially when you're standing here
Freezing cold, the rain is pouring scenery is getting boring
Frozen hands, it makes you think
Someone fetch another drink
Someone fetch another drink

Whisky coffee, rum laced tea, anything to warm up me
Feet are freezing, knees are knocking, blimey, is this weather shocking
Damp the clothing, dripping hair, home is close - we're almost there
Lots of room to moor, that's handy
Hug the fire, where's the brandy
Hug the fire, where's the brandy

In the summer it's much better
(Mind you, couldn't get much wetter!)
When you're damp at least it's warm
Steaming through the August storm
At least there won't be queues for hours
Hire boats don't work locks in showers
Forecast says it's turning fine
Happy days, now where's the wine
Happy days, now where's the wine

Summer heat at last we feel
Long time coming, is this real?
For each lock we have to wait
As tourists savour each lock gate
"Well," they say, "what's the hurry?"
Job-end deadlines causing worry
How much longer are we here?
Pass me out another beer
Pass me out another beer

Getting there is hit & miss
Ask again why we do this
Nothing short of being barmy
Tougher sometimes than the army
Lengthened days & shortened nights
Rotten weather, endless flights
Why we do this? Let me think
Pass me out another drink!
Pass me out another drink!

Joey Reprise - Part Three

In new millennium purpose has changed
Workboats are rare and for leisure exchanged
Widebeams as liveaboards, time rearranged
Modern canal life leaves history estranged

Look to the future and what lies ahead?
Boats mainly houses, no journey to tread
Use, but use wisely with care in your head
Another decline could see waterway dead

Iron to Irony Reprise

I am iron
I am warm
And living
And I am from another time

But if life is kind
I will outlive
My custodians
In hope
Of gentle handover
To future days

For I am iron
I am warm
And living;
And I am from another time

Keep The Joeys Moving - Reprise

So time has moved along and again we changed the song
And life is very different for a Joe
An office, or a shed, maybe fit a proper bed
And these days there's not so far for us to go
Not so much of hauling as the neighbours come a calling
Your daily job a stationary rut
And on your leisure days you can think of all the ways
That you can get your joey moving on the cut

So off we go again, different purpose now to then
And her engine may be inboard, fitted new
The odds against the steerer, it couldn't be much clearer
That most folk out there just haven't got a clue
There's kayaks and canoes, folks with flip flops and no shoes
And designer dogs replace the faithful mutt
More crowded now than ever, it doesn't seem so clever
Now your joeys stuck in traffic on the cut

What would the Gaffer say if he saw his boats today
And the pace of work would make him blow a fuse
I guess he'd sack us all, health and safety up the wall
And he'd laugh when told he'd go to court and lose
In getting sentimental for times which seemed more gentle
Old plodding Ned whose stable doors are shut
The good old ways are gone as the times keep moving on
From when we kept the joeys moving down the cut

CHORUS
Keep the joeys moving, keep the joeys moving
Keep the joeys moving down the cut
Keep the joeys moving, keep the joeys moving
Keep the joeys moving down the cut

**The circles of life coincide -
as the people and boats
become one**

Circles

Chorus
Never quite touching
But somehow connected
The dance begins
Moving through life
The unstoppable flow of the tide
Through high and low
And the friendships which grow
Last forever

**As the circles ....
.... Coincide**

Deep in mid-winter, there was the sweet smell of summer
And I was the one who guided the light on the road
Watching the pheonix rising again from the ashes
A dangerous game or request, 'cos I'll bring out your worst and your best
There's no question why, for the eagle will fly
'till there's nothing we haven't confessed

So tell me a secret you never knew you knew
And are you the wise one who always sees me through?
Or are you the devil leading me astray?
Chasing rainbows that never, never, never, never fade to grey

Living For Today

Watch me now, it's been so long
Since I smiled within a song
But now, I know how
I'm not gonna change 'cos now I'm living for today

Watched the moon in candlelight
Found it easier to get it right in the sunlight
Where shadows aren't hiding in the night
Been too long in the shade
Raised my head and found I'd got it made
No more hiding, feeling alone
Life's an easy game

One by one we all fall down
Get back up, don't let it get you down
You are the best now at what you are, don't ever give in
Follow dreams, lose your sorrow
Every sunset brings a brand new day tomorrow
Don't be afraid now
Stay the distance you'll find you're on your way

Janul grew up in the Black Country as the canal system was heading towards a decline. Much has changed.

Writing songs and poetry from the age of 12, she had to wait for over 40 years to develop the broader view of canal life which she talks about so enthusiastically today. The show is loosely scripted, adding a diverse layer to each performance and meaning that you never know which tale she will tell to which audience.

Living full time on the canal, Janul has secured her place through working on and owning a variety of canal boats, which have indulged her lifelong passion.

After over 4 decades of varied boating including large trip boats, tugs and coalboats, as well as owning the successful RYA training school, Canal Experience, there are many incidents of hilarious and almost unbelievable content to relate.

Janul's performance has a good deal of passion relating to the boats, life and a changing world, with just a hint of reflection in which she joins the modern world, the future and more than a few past experiences together.

Please join in as the show comes to a venue near you. Mostly donations, so everyone is welcome.

If you think you have seen JANUL's work before, you may recall seeing some of her canal related books.

They are available from Amazon, most book retailers and signed copies from
https://www.janul.com

jan@janul.com   07850 846495

www.ingramcontent.com/pod-product-compliance
Lightning Source LLC
Chambersburg PA
CBHW051324110526
44590CB00031B/4459